THE MIDDLE KINGDOM

The Middle Kingdom

POEMS, 1929-1944

BY CHRISTOPHER MORLEY

ER MINNET IEMER DESTE BAZ
SWER VON MINNEN ETEWAZ
HOERET SINGEN ODER LESEN

—WALTER VON DER VOGELWEIDE

HARCOURT, BRACE AND COMPANY
1944

A WARTIME BOOK

IN THOUGHT OF
DON MARQUIS
1878-1937

NOTE

These poems seem to the author to appeal for priority among his publishable verse written in the past fifteen years. A good many of them have appeared in magazines or newspapers; some in the pleasurable obscurity of a pseudonym. The happiest adventure of the pseudonym was to receive a letter from a prominent publisher saying that the sonnets were so vigorous why shouldn't the writer try his hand at a novel?

For reprint permissions I thank The *Atlantic, Harper's,* The *New Yorker,* The *Saturday Review of Literature,* The New York *Times,* The New York *Post,* The *Argus Book Shop,* The Chicago *Daily News,* the Columbia University Press, The *American Mercury,* and (with special pride) The *Old Farmer's Almanac.* Also the J. B. Lippincott Company, who have allowed the use of some verse passages from books under their copyright.

C. M.

Roslyn Heights, L. I.
May 5, 1944

CONTENTS

[x]

THE MIDDLE KINGDOM

WHILE REVISING SOME VERSES

Here, in a sky so pure, weather so sweet
How can a verse endure
Fit to compete?
These were my love of earth, truly confessed:
Broken the word comes forth.
Silence was best.

Song that eluded print, pen still unwet,
Letter that was not sent,
Type never set:
Those, in the hidden wit, nothing can fret.
Silence is exquisite—
And yet . . . and yet . . .

A SONG FOR EROS

If, in days of sullen air,
   Dark with anger, dull with grief,
Merciful and unaware
   There transpire for thy relief
      Lighter mood or cleaner sky—
      Look no further: it is I.

Bandaged close and held apart
   Are thy mortal wounds that bleed,
Yet some subtle healer's art
   Touches on thy secret need:
      What physician, then, to bless?
      I it was, eased thy distress.

Beauty never guessed before
   Universal to the gaze:
Laughter copious to restore
   All the waste of barren days:
      Cistern water turned to wine—
      Yea, these miracles are mine.

Under Zeus' immortal nod
   I am passion undefiled:
I, the child that is a god
   And the god that is a child.
      Canst thou not identify
      Thy magician? It is I.

THE NIGHTPIECE TO HERRICK

O Herrick, parson of my heart
   I'll go to church with thee,
And bear a humble willing part
   In thy sweet liturgy.

The Trinity by thee confessed,
   Thy book of common prayer,
Are Julia's leg, Anthea's breast,
   And Dianeme's hair.

DOGWOOD TREE

Whiteness crept up through the woody veins
   And spread all sudden on the unknowing air—
That should have cured stupidities and pains?
   I could not watch it long. It's rude to stare.

And you made nothing of it, ere it vanished?
   That naked beauty of your own dear Day,
Life's whitest body—
   I was grateful and astonished,
But what was there to say?

A toss of foaming like the crystal shatter
   Of a bursting wave, in magic pause—
And was that all you thought about the matter?
   I wanted to tell *you* how beautiful it was.

DOROTHY

"I made pies in the morning. William went into the wood, and altered his poems."

—DOROTHY WORDSWORTH, *July 28, 1800.*

William went into the wood: the poem needed revising
   (Probably he put back what she had suggested first)
Dorothy watched the oven to see that the loaf was rising,
   Copied some Chaucer for him, and cooked and sewed and nursed.

William was out of spirits; Coleridge tramped from Keswick
   (Said his bowels were bad, and the wind made his eyes so sore)
Dorothy read their poems aloud, and gave them physic,
   Quitted her well-earned bed, and slept on the parlor floor.

She wept (she had her reasons); William said she "blubbered";
   She walked the road to Rydal to see if the post went by;
William was reading Congreve, but Dorothy went to the cupboard
   And served the gooseberry pudding, and the homemade giblet pie.

William walked on the mountain; Dorothy planted broccoli—
   William could not "kindle," and had a pain in his head;
Coleridge had a fantod, but bore up well, and pluckily
   Let her broil him a mutton chop and serve it to him in bed.

Coleridge cut his name on stone, and Dorothy kissed the boulder;
   William danced with the daffodils, and took the word from her:
Then he rested, and had his nap leaning against her shoulder—
   Only the very wise would guess whose poems they really were.

AMMONOOSUC

(1938)

There are two streams that bear the name,
One is the Wild and one the Tame;
And on an afternoon we came
    To the Wild Ammonoosuc.

We lay in stupor, sweating, prone
Upon a ledge of sunwarmed stone;
I could not rest for beauty shown
    Beside the Ammonoosuc:

The small pink flower on supple stalk,
The confidential water-talk
As you came down from Moosilauke
    O amber Ammonoosuc.

Unspeakable in rhyme or prose
That moving Now the spirit knows,
The flow that pauses, pause that flows
    So like the Ammonoosuc,

And I, who had escaped from men,
From How and Why and Where and When,
Cried: Take me, make me whole again,
    O blessed Ammonoosuc.

Where her crystal overran it
I lay down in channeled granite;
Braced against the pushing planet
    I bathed in Ammonoosuc.

In that sluice of stream and sun
I dreamed that I and everyone
A whole new ethic had begun
    Inspired by Ammonoosuc.

Refreshed in her, I understand
One truth from A to ampersand:
That every heart in every land
    Has its own Ammonoosuc.

Be then, O secret cataract,
For me both parable and fact;
You gave me what my courage lacked
    O reckless Ammonoosuc.

When all the world moves widdershin
(Half Tory and half Jacobin)
Come pour your mountain freshet in,
    My sweet Wild Ammonoosuc.

The open way has symbols three:
The fire, the stream, the growing tree;
If I grow morbid, say to me:
    Remember Ammonoosuc.

SONNET IN A KNOTHOLE

We idled at our doings, heart and I.
We watched the puddle lose its glaze of frost,
Measured the April in a pale March sky
And saw the birch-tree root all newly mossed.
Filling our fingernails with spring, we raked
And burned and swept, and breathed, and chopped some wood;
And even in that easiness, heart ached
To keep this noon forever, if we could.

But no one guessed (we made no outward stopping)
The sudden woodsman stroke that we incurred
When down through fiber, grain, and knotted wit
The oak of language shivered, cleanly split
By the flashed ax-blade of the perfect word.

We tightened steel to helve, and went on chopping.

VIII

No bird has built an April nest
   More instinctive than my rhyme,
A hidden coil where thought can rest
   In lonely or in stormy time.

I weave for you these twigs and straws,
   The casual shreds of every day:
Your love can shelter there for pause
   And, when it needs to, fly away.

I build it hidden, shy, unknown,
   And weatherwise, with simple care.
And even when the bird has flown
   The empty nest will still be there.

HAMPSTEAD COACH

February 3, 1820

He rode to town, that day false-mildest still
In all our treacherous almanac of spring;
My dowsing rod, he thought, a forked quill,
Feels the deep twitch of fresh imagining.
A play for Drury Lane? Or verse diffused
With all St. Agnes' colors (O bright star!)
And if it's good enough to be abused
I'll sign it—like La Belle Dame—*Caviare*.

February filldyke: that night, frost,
The perjured crocus sleeted in the mud
And Hampstead Hill slow-climbed in gale and torrent.
Why, he looks radiant; but the eyes are glossed
With fever.
       "Rode outside? No coat? Good God—"
"Brown, let me see that blood. . . ."
             It's my death warrant."

DISCRETION IN MIDSUMMER

Night left us early, but her sport was shown:
A cobweb handkerchief was on the grass,
Her raindrop crystals on the sassafras,
And after-dinner nutshells on a stone.
Her lipstick stained the rhododendron cone,
Torn gown, her color, blue as poison-glass,
Was in the larkspur. All the birds, en masse,
Were gossiping that if the truth were known . . .

We smoothed the tumbled beds and made all neat,
Squirrels and I. Cleared each betraying sign
(No gardener will mention all he knows).
Put on your tails, I said, and be discreet:
For we were due on the receiving line
To greet a well-bred debutante, the rose.

END OF AUGUST

How gradual, gradual the dark came on:
If ever there were silence, that was it.
My freshcut grass smelled sweet as cinnamon,
I felt myself beginning to forget.
Almost equal in such dim desire
Were things I never won and things I lost
Till, chattering voltage like a broken wire
The wild cicada cried, Six weeks to frost!

Then dark was damnable. Night was too clear:
The trees no shelter, for the stars burned through;
And now this morning, when I first go out
What do I see, poised in the western sheer?
Curved downward like a hooked and leaping trout,
Waning, the moon we had when it was new.

BASAL METABOLISM

He put his slippers high up on the bureau
Beyond the puppy's reach (perhaps a fable
Of education?); oiled his workroom table;
Found a picture, snapped one night of zero
(Moon in a crystal tree); remembered winter
And chopped more wood; poured the cat a saucer;
Resolved to read some Virgil and some Chaucer;
Then singed a needle and pried out a splinter.

He watched the agile antics of a bird,
But darkness was implicit in blue air—
Blood thrummed his ears, and far inside he heard
(Like a child at night) step—step—on the stair.
Then lunch.
       He fell asleep.
               It seems to me
Just Miscellaneous Sensibility.

ALLERGIES

O.K. . . . then we'll talk turkey. No more crap.
There is a me, old son, you never guessed,
Who wants no others' problems in his lap
And has short patience with the social pest.
Among the boys I specially detest
Are who suppose I'm loafing when I'm thinking,
Who pride themselves for hair upon the chest
And think you must be drunk because you're drinking.

Add minor hates: the vinculated *g*
("Long Gyeland") or the h dropped out of *human*,
The difficulty of getting kedgeree,
And pointed crimson fingernails on woman.
Or speakers who end "Thank you." (Hypocrites!) . . .
I've blown off steam. I'm better. End of blitz.

ALEXANDER POPE, 1688-1744

POPE, who loved his rhymes in duplicates,
Chose couplets also for his mortal dates:
Born '88, precisian to the core,
Died, of exactitude, in '44.

Duplex himself, both wasp and honey-bee:
The wasp whose sting was immortality;
The bee whose nectar, sugared in the cyst,
Could turn to fury in a paper nest.

When Pope lit on the bare hide of a dunce
He did not need to do so more than once.
It was no use to rub the place with soap.
The only lucky fools were born since Pope.

Most perfect mind in English, he had fun:
Assassin and embalmer, both in one.

THE WATCHMAN'S SONNET *

The night was heavy: thunder in suspense.
The shelves were gloom wherever one might look—
No darkness anywhere is quite so dense
As that shut up in a forgotten book.
Even the watchman at the timeclock desk
(Imaginative in his own despite)
Saw wisdom as a wavering grotesque,
A cone of shadow barely tipped with light.

Since men learned print, no night is wholly black,
But dawn was torrent, and fog followed rain.
Sideways he saw a flash, a speeding thing—
Lightning? He startled for the thunder-crack,
Then knew what flickered past the window pane:
Daylight, replenished on a bird's wet wing.

* Written, by the "Honorary Night Watchman," for the 50th anniversary of the
Columbia University Press.

RETREAT

I saw a broken soldier in the West
With antique tricorne hat pulled forward low,
His poor old shoulders hunched, his chin on chest
And belt and saber sagged. I saw him go
Reeling and tottering, but still he pressed
In one direction only. Driven so,
A left, a right, mechanical, possessed,
The Guard retreated in the Russian snow.

I looked again: my veteran was gone
Across the frozen wilderness of space,
But somewhere he slogs desperately on
Limping, and accoutrement awry,
Like Napoleon's marshals in disgrace—
Orion, that great straggler of the sky.

TWO SONNETS TO THEMSELVES

I knew that I was lonely. I allowed
I'd face it: and then what I needed most,
The power of words, came on me. So I'm proud
And celebrate a private Pentecost.
Yes, proud as hell. What man has been more fain
Of sweet and savage and all gust of earth,
Or watched the curly shorthand of the brain
Take down such patterns of outrageous mirth.
Since you are wise and generous and kind
I tell you this. I tell it to you only,
But I am proud that others too may find
Our beauty serviceable when they're lonely.
I could not be so proud unless I knew
How humbly I can tell it all to you.

You like to laugh? Sure, I can make you laugh,
And, if you wished it, I could make you cry.
You like to put an act on, and get half
Way through, and be caught up with? So do I.
Then we are mutual of each other's mood,
The target and the missile both in one:
Joy in pursuit and joy to be pursued,
And—lords of understatement—call it fun.
So we were gay as wine and plain as bread
And wary of the hurt behind the kiss,
And one day in astonishment we said
We never knew that people loved like this.
Now ring the chime, bob major, in our steeple:
That we are Us, and never will be "people."

WISHFUL THINKING

Precariously sits the soul
  Among such queer machineries;
It only has remote control,
  Like college deans in deaneries.

So lobbied and so pressure-grouped
  By dreams, or indigestion,
No wonder Intellect gets pooped
  And simply Begs the Question.

HENCH AND WENCH

Cupid, reproached for lovers' pains,
Has no more conscience than King Kong;
A billion henchmen, he maintains,
And their henchwomen, can't be wrong.

A bow and arrow? Nothing such!
He heaves a golden monkey wrench:
It strips the gear and stalls the clutch—
And how they love it, hench and wench.

DICHOTOMY

I saw no merit in the scheme
  Of Nature's primitive division:
Though sex, they told me, was supreme,
  I held it always in suspicion:
    It seemed too gross, too much imbued
    With propagative purpose crude.

But now, O palinode, confess:
  Dichotomy proves more appealing,
For since I saw you, loveliness,
  I have a wholly different feeling:
    To my astonishment intense,
    Biology makes better sense.

Magnificent is Nature's plan,
  Provocative, ingenious very,
To make a woman and a man
  So mutually necessary:
    Let Beauty flourish her allures—
    I am, appetitively yours. . . .

CHICAGO

How do I hold you, city, in the mind
When my backward memory goes exploring?
An ocean without salt, a gale roaring,
A cruel blackness with a glittering rind.
Luxurious windows along dingy streets,
A rumbling loop of elevated cars,
Forbidding alleys, shadowshining bars,
And every mood from Al Capone to Keats.

Fantastic town, town feminine, town mad,
The town of Panta Rei (or, Everything Goes),
Town packed with comedy like bones in shad
Where even the cop a cuckoo-whistle blows
And in the sky an electric whiskey ad:
A seal that spins the world upon his nose.

SONG·FOR A BARITONE

When autumn dusk was coming soon
   Beyond an amber tree,
I saw a young unmarried moon
   Who turned her cheek to me.

Perhaps because my mood was low
   And frost was in the air,
I thought of girls I used to know
   And how, and when, and where;

Of all delicious escapades,
   The merry and the sad—
Of roving matrons, reckless maids,
   And pretty clothes they had.

And other recollections too
   Made wistful memory stir:
Oh, you—and you—and you—and you—
   How comical we were!

So now, when nights begin to freeze,
   And pious thoughts belong,
I'd like each one to know that she's
   Remembered in my song.

Indeed I wish I could assure
   That group of noble dames
How faithful is their paramour—
   But I forget their names!

BALLADE OF AN OLD FRIEND

"Farewell my book and my devotion"
  When dogwood's white propellers spin,
So quick, while I am in the notion,
  A carnal ballad I begin:
  Come, fair of face and light of shin,
    Toss grievance to the camphor ball—
  A Rousing Snort, a double gin,
    To Chaucer, dearest of them all.

My Cressid, use your sweetest lotion,
  Wear tender silk against the skin,
My chosen child, my Land of Goshen,
  My hoarded bottle in the bin!
  "A weather for to slepen inne"
    Is this, he said, you may recall
  (And said it with his charming grin)—
    Old Chaucer, dearest of them all.

For this particular emotion
  The modern poets sound too thin,
For some are cold and Nova Scotian
  And some distemper us with din.
  O minstrel with a voice of tin,
    Vamoose yourself, and hire a hall—
  I want wise, kindly, masculine
    Dan Chaucer, dearest of them all.

ENVOY

Lover of flesh, who found no sin
  In life's most various festival,
My master and my most of kin,
  Hail Chaucer, dearest of them all.

BALLADE OF A HOROSCOPE

A strong, impulsive, passionate nature . . . self-willed, headstrong, inde-
pendent . . . not an easy person to deal with . . . reason doesn't have any
effect on your emotions . . . a curious twist causes tension to turn into
inertia . . . instability. . . .
                    —*Heaven Knows What* (a book of horoscopes)

Astrology we sing!
   Though people don't adore us
The horoscope's the thing
   That makes allowance for us:
   Our resolution's porous?
      Our morals vertigo?
   We had the Sun in Taurus,
      The Moon in Scorpio.

To both extremes we swing
   While moderates deplore us—
Now full of visioning,
   Now tough as dinosaurus.
   At least they'll not ignore us,
      And if our tastes are low,
   We had the Sun in Taurus,
      The Moon in Scorpio.

Then let the Scorpion sting
   And let the Great Bull gore us:
An alibi we bring
   For conduct indecorous;
   Yes, when our mothers bore us
      The stars were thus and so—
   We had the Sun in Taurus,
      The Moon in Scorpio.

ENVOY

O Zodiac, restore us
   When friends are shocked. You know
*We had the Sun in Taurus,
   The Moon in Scorpio!*

SONG IN A DENTIST'S CHAIR

(Which I Wish Someone Would Set to Appropriate Music)

All joys I bless, but I confess
    There is one greatest thrill:
What the dentist does when he stops the buzz
    And puts away the drill.

His engine hums along my gums
    Its excavating drone,
I salivate and gurgling wait
    Vibrating to the bone.

Oh, will he save this tooth concave
    Or will he now decide
To grind away some more decay?
    He murmurs, *Open wide.*

So I must feel the burring steel,
    The hot and fragile twinge,
And mutely bide till he push aside
    The bracket on its hinge.

But will he swerve across that nerve?
    I wonder, gagged, agape:
He sees me gulp and spares the pulp—
    My God, a close escape!

The creosote is in my throat,
  I weep against my will;
My nostrils itch, sensation which
  I can't relieve until
He stops the buzz and packs in fuzz
  And puts away the drill.

I grant the bliss of love's warm kiss
  Or wealth, or fame, or skill:
These I esteem but yet I deem
  There is one greater thrill—
When he stops the buzz, as at last he does,
  And puts away the drill!

TELEVISION

Through her eyes, the far beholder,
    I try to look, and so make clear
The little things I might have told her
    And what she'd see if she were here.

O may she also, tender doxy,
    Our visual faculties combine
And use her pretty eyes by proxy
    To see all Other Men through mine.

IN A SECOND-HAND BOOKSHOP

What waits me on these shelves? I cannot guess,
  But feel the sure foreboding; there will cry
A voice of human laughter or distress,
  A word that no one needs as much as I.

For always where old books are sold and bought
  There comes that twinge of dreadful subtlety—
These words were actual, and they were thought
  By someone who was once alive, like me.

"A NIGHT AT AN INN"

(Edward John Moreton Drax Plunkett, 18th Baron Dunsany—*Who's Who*)

To BEDWARD, says EDWARD.
I'm on, cries JOHN.
It helps to shorten the night, quoth MORETON.
Just a glass of port, to relax, says DRAX.
And now we've drunk it, mumbles PLUNKETT,
Come on, old zany.
And so all five, with yawns and snorts,
Having partaken their Cinque Ports,
Are merged in bed as LORD DUNSANY.

PROPRIETOR

In my woodlot, one warm afternoon,
Was a long downward streak, so arrowy and sinuous
It looked continuous.
It flowed, it poured, it was gone,
Almost an illusion, a sham
Like a line in a diagram.

Clean as a flume it sped,
With a pinpoint eye in its head,
And hid unsociable in the honeysuckle brake
But I was proud, and said
"My snake—*My* Snake!"

DEATH OF A PANDA

("Of an ailment not yet identified."—N. Y. *Times*, May 14, 1941)

Among your zoological memoranda
Record the obit of our New York panda.
The cause of her decease how to determine?
Nostalgia? Faulty diet? Obscure vermin?
Of air-conditioning? Or being stared at?
Or no other mammal to be paired at?

Contortionist in fur, Pierrette and nun,
Eyes rounded with demure Mongolian fun
And pleased as paunch, she could not bear the torment:
A weltblitz is too much for a simple varmint.
So died the world's most innocent of critters,
A victim of the universal jitters.

RONDO FOR KING WHIRL

". . . Else Whirl is King."

—H. L. B. in *The Commonweal*.

Sing roundelay for old King Whirl
Whose temperament is nervish:
Spinning Jenny is his girl,
His premier is a dervish.

When pleased he cries aloud, "That's Tops!"
He never knew what No meant;
And every instant something pops—
Oh, never a dull moment.

To give us bread and circuses
His crops are in rotation:
He says the public passion is
Perpetual gyration.

So Time is mere tick doloroo,
And I O U just vowels,
And if your head feels split in two
You ring for more hot towels.

Sing old King Whirl, balletomane
Without a trace of static:
Reproached, he says with look of pain
"Oh, let's not be lymphatic!

"Strap on the skate, accelerate
Ere jealous Time ungland us,
The motto of the Perfect State
Is *Non sufflaminandus*.

[35]

"You sorrypuss, poor Such-and-such,
Your nerves and knees are flaccid—
Avaunt the gloomy Hamlet touch
Of too much Yorick Acid."

So old King Whirl in Trebizond
Appointed, just to spite us,
As consort, good Queen Dizzy Blonde;
As patron saint, Saint Vitus.

SEACOAST OF INDIANA

O nerve of thought, alert, aware,
That strips the moment naked-bare
And lives in double, Here and There—

That equals hunger with disgust,
Surrenders everything on trust
And begs for speech because it must—

A dune of living sand, ablaze,
Climbed in the utter noon of days
For body's cry and mind's amaze—

The silver needle through the skein,
The pain hidden within the pain,
The sickness whereof none complain.

Forecast for tomorrow: rain.

SIR KENELM

Now with a shout of joy I let you go:
Nothing, henceforward, can our triumph vary;
We have been worthy of the moon and snow
And made long summer of our January.
Such tender incidence of chances odd
As saintlier lovers might have wished to die in
We've had; and also, O my God, my God,
What clear and cruel dusks to say good-by in.

And when we're old—if ever we *are* old—
And miracles once secretly impressed
Are evident on the brow for men to see,
There'll be some print there, subtle to behold,
Of all we knew and felt and learned and guessed
In days when I loved you, and you loved me.

REQUIESCO ON RIVERSIDE

When convoys blow, and I can't sleep,
I count a different kind of sheep,
Reviewing those who lay awake
For imagination's sake,
For some maggot in the brain.
Shakespeare, Swift, and Keats and Blake
Lone and vigilant have lain;
Hazlitt, Melville, Lamb, Thoreau,
Henry James, Boccaccio,
Tortured in the shameless hours,
Doubtful of their godlike powers,
Made a light, to help ignore
Moonlight squared upon the floor;
Or, in solitude still deeper,
Shirked the heat of some near sleeper.
Bunyan, Dr. Johnson, Walt,
Misogynist or nympholept,
Whate'er the pain, whate'er the fault,
Up their shins the languor crept
And, eventually, they slept.

Now am I these brothers' keeper;
Sisters' too: divesting slow,
The pink, the tawny, and the pale
Prim the linen, palm the covers
(Farewell dishpan! farewell lovers!)
Dorothy Wordsworth, Hester Thrale,
Virginia Woolf, Virginia Poe;
Horse-faced Evans, dark and sallow
With her hair spread on the pillow,
Emily Dickinson, Emily Brontë
(*Noctis equi, currite lente!*)—
Girls that every poet knows:
Herrick's Julia, Landor's Rose,
Louis Stevenson's firebrand Fanny,
Tom De Quincey's Opium Annie,
Sidney's Stella, Burns's Mary—
Prioress, voluptuary.

Girls of learning, men of science
Tread my causeway of the giants,
Visualized, revered, and numbered
In their image as they slumbered:
Dormouse curl or downward sprawl,
Nothingness is on them all.
Tired of love or tired of drinking,
Tired of fighting, tired of swinking,
The accursèd or the blest
Momentarily at rest.
Chaucer, alderleefest Geoff,
Full eight hours is blind and deaf
To mimicry; old wiseabed,
Sleeps more peaceful than the dead.

Mine own sweethearts! Noble crew,
They sleep well.
                              And I shall too.

THE SPOKEN WORD

(December, 1942)

A voice was speaking, known to many ears:
The voice of Toil and Tears, that never yet
Promised us anything but Blood and Sweat—
That day our Second Front was Radio.

As we tuned the wave-band to and fro,
Listeners from Brisbane to Bengazi could hear the Naazie
Struggling on the fringe of tone,
Trying to jam the air with guttural of his own.
Only one word came rasping through:
They'd have kept silent if they knew,
They'd have been wiser if they had—
The word was *Stalingrad*.

It's December night and a gale is blowing,
The trees are loud with going,
A trailing ivy rubs and squeaks on the pane—
I wonder what it's like in the Ukraine,
Or the Bend of the Don—or the Bend of the Styx?
Or where those Russian girls climb through a pile of bricks
From their cellar underground.
The sky's a black throat of sound, the tree-tops roar,
The ragged wind is thrashed in syllables,
The naked scaffold of the oak takes voice, and cries
Turin . . . Corregidor . . .
Dunkirk . . . Bataan . . . Tobruk . . . Coventry . . . Singapore.
My sibil ivy hisses on the glass,
Whispers 'They shall not pass,'
I hear the Cossack blizzard blow
Its three-toned chord, harsh, proud, and sad
The name of steel: the name of *Stalingrad*.

Words are a blessing in the head,
Secret to think, difficult to be said.
O spoken word, come clean. Say what you mean,
Be hopeful, humble, and exact; servant of fact.
For your destiny immense, O spoken word, make sense.
However instantaneous you appear,
It's always later There than Here.

Not long ago I shot the breeze with Chaucer
(Best friend the English language ever had)
Up to his House of Fame. This he imagined
An over-all control-room or Blue Network,
A listening post for all the talk of men
(To be fully informed, read Chaucer every morning).
There are new voices now in the House of Fame,
And modes of speech original as Chaucer's:
"Fellow Amarricans," when Indiana
Doubles the r's that Churchill couldn't say,
And Tennessee's douce Appalachian drawl
Gives the assu'ance of the govvement
Poe-litical and spiritchle resohces
Will relieve large potions of the world.
Or, dialing the B.B.C. at midnight,
"Our bommahs crossed the Alps."
But Chaucer shames me: "There's diversité
In English, and in form of speche is chaunge."
Peace will be treated in all sorts of accents—
And *Stalingrad?* Those best can say it
Who lived in cellars rather than betray it.

Ink will not write the history of that year,
Begun and ended in the smokes of burning—
One shamefullest of all, when shame was ours:
The rubber-smelling stink that spread the city
Where *Normandie,* fouled on our very doorstep,
Sprawled like a rotting whale.
Poets grew shrill, and History went mad,
But on her private memorandum pad
She wrote the one word
Stalingrad.

"FLUCTUAT NEC MERGITUR"

(June, 1940)

The Paris that I set my heart upon
Can be defiled: The Luxembourg, les Halles,
The little Café-bar de la Sorbonne,
The Cent Mille Chemises, the Etablissements Duval.
Sacked and shattered, maybe, but not ceded,
Town that made thinking feel, and feeling think—
She has a motto to recall when needed:
I may make heavy weather, but not sink.
Suppose the Louvre and Notre Dame were cindered,
In rubble every bookstore and café,
Yet Paris is a city in the mind.
In every good man's thinking you will find
Her lights; and not blacked out and not surrendered
A sign that says, *Ici on parle français.*

AROUND THE CLOCK

"If the German people despair,
I will not be sorry for them."

—ADOLF HITLER, November 8, 1943.

1

Sickness of heart,
  Cold rains that sting—
The time is short
  Till fatal spring.

Speak unreckoned,
  Without revise:
Every second
  Someone dies.

What might the right word be worth?
A million lives on April earth?

A word of missile
  To aim and hit
Wherever the gristle
  Is closest knit;

A word for print
  And a word by air
To plow and plant
  Like a steely share—

Germans, I tell you frank and fair,
There is only one word.
                  The word *Despair*.

2

Drink deep the bitter dose.
Translate it for yourselves—*Verzweiflung? Hoffnungslos?*
Hopelessness is now your only hope.
So many years you savaged and blasphemed,
Corrupted all that patient men had dreamed,
Turned speech to gibberish—
You have your neurotic wish.
Truth, crazed by twenty years of double-talk,
Take up your bed and walk.
Let Truth declare
Your single word, *Despair*.

3

Run, panic word, in every German mind:
Poison the weary nerve and speed the sickness.
After the frenzy comes the horrible weakness.
Who says you this word *Despair?*
It greets you from behind,
But you look and there's no one there.
Anonymous from the sky
You hear it multiply;
Stark on the eastern wind, or salt on the Frisian tide.
The belly loosens and the guts divide.
Print rolls it with a million-metaled tongue:
Your old remember it well,
And your young had no chance to be young.
It is tapped in the telephone wire,
Chokes the kitchen fire, whistles in the plumbing:
The word is coming, coming.
It hums in the radio,
It tiptoes up the stair—
Your word: Despair. Despair.
Cold on the limbs below,
Hot vomit in the skull,
A frost-and-fever spell.
Your word. *Despair*.

4

The speed of a word in flight
  All other speed can mock:
Worse than bombing day-and-night
  Is the Word-Around-the-Clock.

Blacker than bread you had,
  More terrible than the Ruhr,
Crueler than Stalingrad,
  Total, without cure,

Is your own heart's disgust—
  And the Leaders do not care.
This is your only trust:
  To quit. To cease. *Despair*.

5

Heavy, heavy over your head,
Festung Europe,
Doubt becomes dread,
Despair comes nearer.
Read what the junglings scrawl
Chalked around the town:
K. D. F. the youngster scribbles,
Even Goebbels
Knows it doesn't mean Strength Through Joy
But *Kaput Durch Fuehrer*.

There was so much handwriting on the wall
That even the wall fell down.

6

Words return as the years revolve:
We have one, born of a nation's woe;
Sharp as the beveled ax, tough as the hickory helve.
Ours is *Resolve*. "We highly resolve . . ."
The clock strikes twelve
And another American, known as Walt,
Pitiful, as they say, to a fault,
Was a man who never dressed wounds with salt
    And never moved Uptown.
When your Misleaders, fleeing or fled,
Have cast you out, hear what was said
By this good fellow, long since dead:—
"O despairer, here is my neck;
    By God, you shall not go down!"

7

We have drawn the sword
    For a Peace to trust;
It will be hard
    But also just.

It is not to be had
    By wish devout;
Peace has got to be
    Sweated out.

You who have seen
    What men can bear,
Come; come clean;
    But first, *Despair*.

TOULEMONDE DESIPIENT

In this life so slippery
Dulce est desipere.
What are the joys of men?
Enumerate them, then.
Ink that runs from the pen
And forms unbidden the desiderate word;
Scraps of conversation overheard;
Swimming after sweat;
Driving a car;
Remembering the name of one unexpectedly met;
The first cocktail at the bar.
The first warm sun in March;
Collars without starch;
Finding a rare edition;
The dawning dim suspicion
That dame likes me: I think we might go far.

Making a full house from a pair;
Switching comedians off the air.
Among the pleasures particularly man's
Are: mushroom soup in cans;
Old brown shoes well shined;
The laughter hidden in the mind;
Days when everything seems funny;
The return of long-loaned money;
Full appreciation of some art
(Whether hockey or Hokusai);
A bad cold nursed with rock-and-rye;
Hitching the horse behind the cart;
Believing in your soul
The part is greater than the whole.

The joy of being warm
By firelight on a night of storm;
Moonlight when it stipples
Long Island Sound in ripples.

The footlights glowing on the curtain
On a First Night of your own;
Remembering, though uncertain,
A number on the phone;
Books on which there's a hoodoo
Because no one likes them as well as you do,
Or very few do.

The fun that people miss
By being prim and priss
(Also the snags they strike
By doing too much what they like);
Morning papers and orange juice on breakfast tables;
The almost vanished smell of livery stables;
Engines that go by steam
(For pistons and cranks,
Oh Lord, my thanks);
The curiosities of dream;
An unexpected Valentine;
Spaghetti and red wine.
Hot towels at the barber's;
Tea and bread-and-butter in English arbors;
Falling asleep with a detective story
(One that's both intelligent and gory).

The feeling of a day when nothing has to be done:
No appointments, absolutely none,
Just to loiter along the shelves
Reintegrating all one's various selves;
And then, when everyone's in bed,
The silence overhead.

His blue morocco slippers donned,
What evenings then had Toulemonde.

TOULEMONDE: THE GOLDEN GERM

(Or, Dogs Don't Bark at the Milkman)

Now . . .
Coffee drunk, and mail collected,
Newspaper read and telephone not ringing
(Alliteration chiming in the skull)
Comes verse, the always mischievously candid.
She has to wait
Until compulsories abate
But when the tides of rumbling prose
Are out, along the elastic beach she goes
Picking up shells and sharkteeth that were stranded.
She and I, each other's each,
Are never lonely on that beach.
Our joy to reaffirm
I sing you the Golden Germ.

Here, in this clear February pause,
Tarry, forenoon blue; mind, catch up, draw level
And all else go to the devil.
O sweet brief month, O February
Of ills examined and health preferred,
O mystical preliminary
Of Word made flesh—and flesh made word.
O earliest thought of naked Spring,
How pink she lounges after bath
Unconsciously exhibiting
Her slopes of cream, her bronzy swath:
But be not tattletale in Gath:
When goddesses have nothing on
We nuncupate, and leave to wrath
The publishers in Askelon.
Though Spring smell lavender as Yardley
Need I tell the world? Well, hardly.

But the moon's at full and crystalline
To chandelier Saint Valentine
And telephone girls in fiscal choir
Sing western unions over the wire:
Sentimental Uncle Sam'll
Walk a mile for a friendly mammal
And physicists recall with cheers
Magdeburg's twin hemispheres:
So unaborted
By things I've seen, and heard reported
(Even the fate of the Escorial
Or this morning's editorial)
I keep my faith in the absurd
Where Life by Laughter is escorted.

This February pause . . .
I've so indulged my proclivity for activity
That just because
I'm happily alone, not answering the phone
And plainly trying to think, I feel almost caitiff,
As though I were shirking, not working;
As though I ought to be dictative, acknowledging letters
Or rush-arounding
(More hounded against, I swear, than hounding)
In a state of nettlerash and jitters.
That's what life does to you if you let it.
A wise man once wrote down (I don't forget it)
Three rules of conduct, fit to be triple-starred:
One, Don't work too hard;
Two, Don't chew your pills but swallow them;
Three, Tell 'em all to go to hell.
He said well,
And I try to follow them.

The sun slants round my Palais de Rumine:
Today's no landscape soft in aquatint
But stenciled sharp on twig and bright horizon;
Clear and bold and crude, like a cartoon.
We've had our morning flush of printers' Epsom,
The world is innocent with busy trade
Till evening papers try again to rouse ·
Man's easy rage or sluggish merriment
And swell my copious glands of disbelief.
The Editor perhaps is wise and pensive:
It isn't he who writes those heads offensive:
The man who has to write the ramping headline
Is under the alarum of a deadline—
A deadline is where something dies
And you know what. Well, life is compromise.

The danger time for thought is moody noon:
Why rub the nerve to persevere for truth?
Most are not interested; why should they care?
(Longer than he lived was Lincoln dead
Before men chose to hear what life he led).
In the hour of apathy and phlegm
We fall back on our saddest apothegm:
"Men are most useful if they do not know,
And what's by all believed is rarely so;
Your dearest doctrine, if the crowd it moves,
Turns inside out and rapidly disproves."

I didn't mean to be so desultorious:
I'm forgetting the Golden Germ.
Staphylococcus is the technical term,
Staphylococcus aureus;
So called because it looks like a bunch of yellow grapes,
But, if annoyed, a Tarzan of the Apes.
Some quite casual boil or scratch
May chance a golden germ to hatch
(If I'm vague in my bacteriology
I make apology)

Perhaps your armpit begins to hurt,
And a vein of fever runs up under your shirt,
Then the doctor sees that his knives are sterile
And your whole arm's in peril.

Then you're not so keen about autonomy
And prefer a planned economy.
Free competition doesn't seem so right
Between *staphylococcus* and phagocyte:
Come, physician! Put my hand in poultice,
Give me a drug in which some healing volt is,
Come antibodies, sulfanilamide!
Up Doctor Jekyll, down with Mr. Hyde!

If this should be the end, it seems a pity:
Gosh, everything was such fun, I hate to leave it;
Loving the world, I'm sorry to bereave it—
And I never wrote my book on New York City. . . .
But the phagocytes, when the other bug gets near 'em
Evolve protective lymph, a yellow serum,
And after several days that try the soul
The trouble's in control.

While your friends are saying how they'll miss you
You're granulating epithelial tissue;
And grateful to the doctor, you thank God he's
On the side of the antibodies.
But not till after you've grown a new epiderm
Do you philosophize the Golden Germ.
Your chance for this little metrical defiance
You owe, most likely, to unboasting science.
Though the conclusion shock us
I'm afraid it's true:
God esteems *staphylococcus*
As much as he does me or you.
This, in case we never knew it,
We better make our minds up to it.
Occasionally it is man's mission
To regulate free competition.

Fact is fact and will be so
Whether Congress sits or no;
Whether you silk or whether you cotton use
The squares of the legs are the squared hypotenuse.
Well-trained dogs, of whatever ilk,
Don't growl at the man who brings the milk.
Truth, like milk, arrives in the dark
But even so, wise dogs don't bark.
Only mongrels make it hard
For the milkman to come up the yard.

Most of all men, I adore
Who tells me what I knew before
And with such tact that we agree—
Not I with him, but he with me!

Thoughts of this general complexion
Came from a Golden Germ infection.
The lovely day passed unaware:
I went to taste the sunset air—
Already Orion's Belt was there.

TOULEMONDE: INTERMEZZO

Here is a song (O dry those tears)
In honor of man's Middle Years—
Unmusical, more like a shout;
But what's the yodeling about?
It's *fun* to grow old . . . if the guts hold out.

Steward?—Steward! Another snort
While I make my interim report.
My gums recede, my belly pouts,
I feel mysterious pangs and gouts
And frequent philosophic doubts.
On flights of stairs my heart goes poop,
I pant and palsy when I stoop—
The woes of flesh no man avoids:
If it isn't flu it's hemorrhoids,
But sagged in front or tweaked behind
All the more ecstasy I find
In the employment of the mind.

Still, thank God, are gorgeous days
When thought kindles to a blaze
On some unearned chrysostom phrase,
Or, with equal pleasure, sags
Upon unmentionable gags—
O brothers, savor them while we may—
What *is* Man, think you, by the way?
Crude actor in a noble play
Or supremely skilled performer
In a dull farce like *Fair and Warmer?*

I had my eras, one by one;
Each was dear, each had its fun,
But man must learn, or his name is mud,
To relish the ebb as well as the flood.
Even in all this woe, we guess,
Are growing pains for the U.S.
Global citizens began it
When Men-about-town became Men-about-planet.
Just now, in partisan catalepse,
Rather wavering are our steps
But all depends on the will-to-think—
Steward! Did you forget that drink?
Plain water, if you please; not Schweppe's.

O lovely lonely lucid hours
When thought swings up to its full powers,
When ego, fantailed like a peacock
Can find the needle in the haycock
And hold the needle's eye and thread it—
Is that millennium? You said it!
When body, mind, and mood congrue
Then nuts for totem and taboo:
There may be very pleasant sins
Not far from Where Taboo Begins.
Beyond the simple cokes of youth
Is also wormwood, or vermouth.

I like to see The Boys grow older:
In face deep-lined or threadbare shoulder
Character shows; and in the grain
Fortune, good or bad, comes plain—
Some who couldn't hold the pace,
Some who sank without a trace
By drink or dames; or worked like hacks
Till economics swung the ax.

Such godhead humors are assured
To the reasonably matured;
Such dexterities defensive,
Pleasures brief but so intensive.

We have learned to flee from bores,
Not to eat green apple-cores,
Find mercy in our humble chores
And watch new tides wash up the shores
Where we had spread, in prose or rhyme,
Our blueprints on the sands of Time.

To disregard all Sacred Cows,
Enjoy occasional carouse,
To know where food and drink agree,
To bid the prude go climb a tree;
Be slow in matters controversial,
Turn off the radio commercial,
Shun grand opera like the pox,
Be dubious of the ballot box,
Defer a little, if we can,
The Century of the Common Man
When everything we most revere
Will get less honor year by year.

And so, oldtimers, you and you
Who drudge these middle decades through
(Often without enough support
Since shirt-tails have been cut so short)
We've raised our kids and paid our tax
And mumbled our rebellious cracks,
We often Took It on the snout.
But also we could Give It Out.
We played our numbers in life's bingo
And, in contemporary lingo,
This is epitaph enough:
We laughed and cursed and loved—And Stuff.

Yes, loved, and lost, and loved some more
And pray there still is love in store
(Short-circuiting Eve's primal curse
By Cupid's lend-lease in reverse)—
Why not drink to Eve, God bless her,
Before our teeth go on the dresser:

Eve whose praise we have established
In verses prudently unpublished,
Eve with cramps or Eve at prayers,
Eve no matter what she wears
From bobbysocks to Bali bra,
From puberty to grandmamma.
See, with eye not too serene,
The *bas bleu* or the ballerine,
Goddess, matron, nymph, and quean.

Boys, methought we did God's bidding
(Which I really mean, no kidding).
Caroled in my long hot bath,
Sang: Belike the time still hath
Foremath besides aftermath;
Sherlock Holmes the truth well put—
Watson, game is still afoot . . .

Overheard a child say, *"Hark!
The Old Man, whistling in the dark!"*

TRANSLATIONS FROM THE CHINESE

REASONS FOR SILENCE

The Old Mandarin has not been heard from
Since he fell off the Gravy Train.

He lost his job as a radio commentator
Because when he quoted anything
He always said "Invert commas . . .
Uninvert commas."
The Vice-president In Charge of Usage
Sacked him, saying
"You can't make mistakes on radio,
It griddles the earth."

He lost his job in a drugstore, too,
Because he thought Sharp & Dohme
Were two different shapes of bra.

CHINESE ACTOR

My favorite actor is the one
Whose name I see
So frequently
On the marquee:
Sat Sun Mon.

ECOLE DES FEMMES

When you kiss my hand, said Pitty Sing,
I get rattled
And don't know what to say.

A well-trained woman
(The Old Mandarin reproached her)
Must learn to conceal
Her disappointment.

RENUNCIATION IN A TELEPHONE BOOTH
BY LADY PRECIOUS STREAM

Though I sometimes disobeyed
  The ration points for steak,
There were calls I might have made
  And did not make.

PRESENTATION COPY

Day after day
You thought I was passing the time
(Or vice versa)
These little poems
Were getting ready for you.

The kind of work I do
No one can tell
(Not even myself)
Whether I'm really working.

ADVICE TOO LATE

Poor Big-Eyes!
Don't, if you can help it,
Fall in love with the Armed Services.
Every time you see the same uniform
You'll be shaken right down to the bilges.

And how, she replied.

PANACHE

Across the street
In the window of a feather merchant
Is a flash of showy colors
And the sign:
MASKS—PLUMES—EFFECTS

My poems are all three.

VALEDICTORY

How I loved that last preface
Of the old poet Thomas Hardy
Where he said
"How I could astonish the young reviewers
By opening this book for them
At certain pages."

OUTCAST IN POKER FLAT

They put away the card table.
I'll lend you some jack to get home,
Said the Old Mandarin;
But a codicil of advice.
Never play poker with the Chinese,
They are saturated
With probability.

DEATH IN THE AFTERNOON

A little time to ourselves
(Said the Duchess's invitation)
And I can pour you a drink.

From a florist's refrigerated showcase
The Old Mandarin brought a bunch of rare tulips
As homage for his hostess.
In the warmth of her parlor
The pink petals soon opened
And in one perfect waxy cup
Lay curled a frozen bee.

Romantic! murmured the Duchess:
Perhaps he's only exhausted.

The flowers kept warming and relaxing
(Likewise the Duchess)
But the bee, the philosopher noticed,
Was permanently dead.
Timidly he reflected:
I'll bet that's just what the tulip said,
One little soothing drink
And some time to ourselves.

My motto, he thought, is *Anxious to please*—
But so was the bee's.

POSTCARD

Don't go hunting for ideas.
Ideas are in the air
Hunting for you.

NO EXERTION

At ten o'clock on a wintry morning
There was already a long line of people
Waiting outside the theater
To see *Jane Eyre*.

What gives, said Chung Stooge, these otiose multitudes
Pack Radio City to see a picture
Who would never dream
Of reading the book?

Sheer and blessed indolence,
Suggested the Old Mandarin.
They can sit warm and quiet
And let it flow over them.
They don't even have to
Turn pages.

ADVERTISEMENT

The Old Mandarin gave up travel
When they began calling it Transportation.
Now, perhaps for patriot reasons,
He stays put, for the Duration.

But O, he cries in a nostalgia,
Is there still that noble billboard
On the islet in the marshes
By the Pennsylvania Railroad
Near the Hudson River tunnel?
Word of prophecy or warning,
New York's promise to the tourist:
BROMO SELTZER FOR HEADACHES.

O, he exclaims,
Maybe,
After the Duration,
One last well-earned Manhattan Migraine!

DANGER SIGNAL

I'm always disturbed
(Said his proper old butler)
When I hear His Excellency
Alone in his workroom
Cackling to himself.
I know he has thought of
Something deplorable.

SOCIOLOGY 4

What is a doctrinaire?
One who has been taught something
Without learning it.

GATE CRASHERS

Every baby vegetable,
Grunted the sweating Victory Gardener,
Is counterfeited by some damned weed
That grows right alongside it.

POACHED EGGS

Wedding Breakfasts a Specialty
Said the menu card
At a secluded seaside hotel.

A delightful place for a wedding breakfast
Said the innocent Old Mandarin.

You wouldn't believe,
Replied the manager,
How many couples
Have enjoyed the breakfast
But didn't bother about the wedding.

ENIGMA

And now, after these tragic bombings,
I'll never see again the ancient landmarks,
Those monuments of old renown.

Don't worry, she said,
You always carry
Your own ruins with you.

TEMPEST 1944

For how many young Americans
Was Shakespeare's stage direction true:
A ship at sea,
And afterwards an island.

PER ARDUA AD ASPIRIN

The post-war world
Will have plenty of headaches.

Exactly, said the philologist:
Migraine in the literal meaning,
Greek *hemi-crania,*
A splitting head.

O planners, study the toxic reactions;
Get ready your drugs and bromides, now.

EAST SIDE WEST SIDE

With another sharptongued mandarin
Rambling far uptown
We discovered
The Guarantee Truss Company.

Let's go in, said my companion,
And ask for a Vice-president.

What would you ask him for, I wonder?
Invisible means of support?

"IL ADMINISTRE SA VERVE"

(—G. LANSON, of Voltaire)

He mumbles an old sheaf of notes,
Of hunches, memos, casual quotes.
Perhaps he'll get a poem from it?
Then, self-abashed, he cries "Why, dammit,
The dog, returning to his vomit!"

GOOD PATIENT

I can always tell if my verses
Are any good, said the Chinese poet.
If they are, they leave me
A little dizzy or faint.

Then you should build up your blood-sugar
Before you do another one,
Said his medical adviser.

A little later I overheard the poet
At a neighborhood bar, saying
"Hi, Steve,
Another one of those blood-sugars."

RIDDLING CONFESSION

On the sill of a ground-floor apartment
When they woke the next morning
Were the padprints of a cat.
In spite of barred windows
Had sneaked in
Dusty little catpaws
Of Time.

Riddling confession,
Said Friar Laurence,
Gets but riddling shrift.

HIS IGNORANCE

The absent-minded Old Mandarin, easily confused,
Gets mixed up by the radio.
For a long time he thought
Kaltenborn was a Russian marshal,
Alkaseltzer a Polish town recaptured,
And *Clippercraft* a Pacific island.

His niece was horrified:
He didn't even know Duke Ellington
From the Duke of Wellington.

CHINESE ORATOR

He usually forgets
The very thing he intended to say
But if he's lucky he may find himself saying
Something much better
Which he never anticipated.

The trouble with cut-and-dried speeches
Is that the speaker dries it
And the audience cuts it.

STUDIES IN DRY VERMOUTH

I'm terrified, she said,
When you do something really unselfish,
For I know too well
That the next time you lose your temper
Either you'll brag about it
Or else curse *me*
For having let you do it.

LITERARY NOTE

He admired a huge beautiful spotted dog
That lay at her feet
And wonderfully enhanced
His mistress's pretty shins.
The old commentator remarked:
"Of course the first Harlequin Dane
Was Hamlet."

STUDENT OF LANGUAGE

Activate, operational, directive,
And even *currently*
Are still going strong
But what became of
Autarky?

AHEAD OF THEIR TIME

When we were students in Paris
(In the year 1912)
After too many drinks
We cried aloud in mischief:
"Vive la *quatrième* Republique!"
A tactless ejaculation
Implying all sorts of trouble
And the gendarmes hustled us
To the jug.

Yet now, la Quatrième Republique
Is what every lover of France
Waits for.

WOMEN'S RESERVE

He learned, at the Naval Training School,
That in order to join the Waves
A girl must be able to hear
Words whispered at 15 feet.

As though any woman couldn't.

HOT LEMONADE

The Old Mandarin
Sneezing fiercely in an attack of flu
Said, If I die tell Henry Wallace
This was the Century
Of the Common Cold.

HEAVY INDUSTRY

To a tycoon in a worldwide business
I made eager suggestion
For political goodwill.

"This company is too big,"
He confessed sadly,
"To do anything significant."

EVERY FORTNIGHT

Just trim off the grizzle
Said the Old Mandarin
When he took his beard to the barber.

Your Excellency, if I take off all the white
There'd be nothing left.

BLUE NETWORK

I'm terribly sorry for Woman
Confided the Old Mandarin; and paused.

They poured him another snifter.
Go on, O. M.—Proceed!

Well, I better put it in parable
And for God's sake don't quote me:
She is never really promoted beyond Receptionist
And in the network of nerves
Spends her life at the switchboard.

ON RIVERSIDE DRIVE

Walking by the river
I see the ships at anchor
Each at a different angle
And I know
The tide is on the turn.

How like young writers!
So quick they feel the changes
In the currents of the time—
Moored between
The flood of E. M. Forster
The ebb of Ezra Pound.

A CASUAL THOUGHT

Just by accident, I suppose,
I am thinking of the world's unpublished poems
And the beautiful imperative reasons
For not publishing them.

BACON'S ESSAYS

O fascicules of felicity,
Portfolios of purge and salt!
I space them out
In the tempo of unconscious verse,
For instance
(The following is transcribed):

Martial men are given to love
As they are given to wine,
For perils commonly ask
To be paid in pleasures.

Or this, which I need to remember:

Why should I be angry with a man
For loving himself better than me?

Prose by any other name
Does not smell as sweet.
His creditors he would sometimes bilk,
But his mind Took Silk.

APPEALED TO HIGHER COURT

Said Counsel: "When your case they try
Tell Truth, whole Truth; no Ands or Buts;
Say Yes or No; don't qualify."

The Court must think I'm nuts:
I'd never take that oath, not I.
What, put my conscience to such straining?
I'd rather lie;
The Truth requires too much explaining.

NEMESIS

In a public house off Fleet Street
(Called The Red Lion)
They ordered another.
The Old Mandarin lifted his glass to his friend,
Saying: I suddenly realize
You and I are the men
My Father warned me against.

GRADUATE SCHOOL FOR MANDARINS

I honor the memory of that wise polymath
Who set a series of searching questions
For his advanced students.
At the top of the paper he wrote:
In this examination
If an exact answer does not suggest itself
There will be value
In an inspired guess.

HYPERSENSITIVE

I've been much too busy to write,
Said Big Eyes;
I've been working on slip-covers.

I wish someone would make a slip-cover for *me,*
Thought the jaded Old Mandarin.
My upholstery is worn through
And all my nerves are exposed.

REMEDY

People who live in glass houses
(Said the Old Mandarin)
Should take a hot bath.
It blinds the windows
With steam.

WEALTHY

The advertisements said it was a book
I couldn't afford to miss.
But I can afford
More than they think.

WARNING

Don't leap to conclusions about people
By what you see them reading.
They may be reading it
(As I do some newspapers)
On purpose to disagree.

PREFACE TO BARTLETT

In poetry there is one test of art:
With whispering stealth, and keeping delicate time,
It creeps into your mind; you find it there.
You are my poem, then, for in my heart
Lovelier than a sonnet you made rhyme
And I had memorized you unaware.

BUT SLIGHTLY SHAKEN

It's good to see you, O. M.—
It's good to be seen, he replied.
How are you these days?
Well, boasted the Old Mandarin
Who had been reading book catalogues:
I'm in good secondhand condition.

GEMMATION IN NOVEMBER

Like trees and shrubs,
I have a false budding
In warm Indian Summer.
Windfall wood in the fireplace
Burns a sweet peppery smell.

THE MIDDLE KINGDOM

The grievance of the Fifth Decade
Is what students of syllogism used to call
An Undistributed Middle.

GRADUATE STUDENT

The loveliest pupil I ever had
Was my little Samoyed soubrette
Who used to cry, after every lecture,
"When does the drinking begin?"
And declared that Bosanquet's *Essentials of Logic*
Was more fun than Sherlock Holmes.

INFERENCE

One of the best and shortest short stories
Was quoted by Bosanquet (from Thackeray)
As an example of Inference from Identity:—
An old abbé, in a party of intimate friends,
Said "A priest has strange experiences;
My first penitent was a murderer."
Later the principal nobleman of the neighborhood
Entered the room. "Ah, Abbé, here you are;
Do you know, ladies, I was the Abbé's first penitent,
And my confession astonished him."

LEGACY

The year has made her will: she left to me
A private purse:
Silver and copper from the dogwood tree,
White gold from a torrent, amber from a pond,
And, for my sadness' sake,
Mountains in a bluescape of beyond.
It might be worse:
These will be useful when I lie awake.

WHERE THE TROUBLE BEGAN

I also (said the Old Mandarin)
Would as lief laugh and loaf
But I'd keep more quiet about it.
The people who really wrecked your civilization
Were those who wrote the Social Columns
In the newspapers.

ESCAPE FROM REALITY

Moonlight and Rum Collins and something by Lentheric
Must have made the sage communicative,
For next morning he asked Poo Pitty Sing:
Did I talk under the ether?

TOOTHPASTE FOR SERPENTS

He reproached the overindulgent parent:
You are like that nature lover
Who put sugar in the birdbath
So that every robin in the neighborhood
Suffers with diabetes.

MONGOLIAN PROVERBS

He is a good writer: the edge of his table is shiny.

* * *

Life has no secrets from the laundress.

* * *

Fifty per cent of the world are women: but they always seem a novelty.

* * *

Nothing is fool-proof when you have a museum-piece fool.

* * *

No one is shocked by a dictionary.

INSCRIPTION FOR A SUN-DIAL

Poetry is the shady sector
Between True North and Magnetic North
Lit never by the sun
But only by the moon—
Gnomon's Land.

UNDERTONE

The very day I set aside for writing
The plumbers came unexpectedly.
I fear through all my verses
You may overhear the clang of pipes,
And voices in the cellar.

"WORDS ARE FOSSIL THOUGHTS"

In the beginning was the Catchword:
It became fresh and dwelt among us.
Columnists used it, and editors
(The old-clothes-men of the mind)
Until it became a Byword.
At last it went to college
And became an Ideology.

SPRUNG RHYTHM

Writing a sonnet
Is like stringing a tennis racquet:
Don't draw the lines too tight at first,
The weather may turn damp.

INTEROFFICE MEMORANDUM

Whenever I call
My friend the Mortician
I always Reverse Charges
For I know he'll even up
In the end.

"A GLASS OF BUCKLE"

Three sociologists with their feet in the cinders
Were defining Civilization.
Civilization (said Groups) is being able
To choose how you will earn a living.
Civilization (said Bunks) is being able
To decide whether you will choose for yourself
Or have the State choose for you.
Civilization (said Yelpers) is where everybody
Works too hard occasionally
And no one works too hard all the time.
Civilization (all three agreed) is having leisure
To attempt to define it.
Meanwhile Civilization was really Old Bill
Who sat quietly with his whiskey
And thought, How young they are.

QUANTUM SUFFICIT

Civilization at its toughest
Allows one day in seven for possible thinking
And it is doubtful if many
Have thoughts enough for more than that.

CONSULT THE AURICLE

A grizzling Mandarin said to himself
In the height of some social uproar:
"I'm really too old
For this sort of thing."
Saying so seemed to prove
To his own satisfaction
That he wasn't.
But as he lay abed afterward
What he thought was riveters next door
Was the pounding in his valves
And his valet rang Room Service
To ask for a stethoscope.

SEDUCED

Now comes after-lunch, the hour of dread.
The Baltimore oriole, Malvolio from Maryland,
Warbles his luscious lyric:
Why do you work, why?
Why? Why work?
There's a new detective story—

A POOR CLIENT

Once I asked a director of Brooks Brothers
(The famous tailors)
Why they never advertised the fact
That their clothes were worn
By Abraham Lincoln.
"We wouldn't dare," he cried in dismay—
"He wore them so badly."

POSTSCRIPT TO A FAMOUS VERSE

But glasses can always be checked
By a girl who's about to be necked.

BEAUTY PARLOR

The homeliest folks, of either sex,
Are those with a crease in the back of their necks.

FLOOD CONTROL

Said the old mystagogue, I admire your Federal projects:
Huge dams to steady the drainage
Of temperamental streams.
But Oh I cry for a TVA
That will check me the greatest river:
The terrible flux of Time.

MANNERS

Always I polish my spectacles
Before going out in a dappled evening.
Let there be no murk on the lenses
When I pay duty to the moon.

FENCES

A Spite-Fence, if I understand your vulgate,
Is a screen to help the jurymen
Keep their minds on abstract testimony
When the defendant is of gracious mold.
But do not, O you well-intending teachers,
Build a Spite-Fence around Literature.
The Muse has pretty legs—
      So let's admire them.

PERISTALSIS

Once, in a fluoroscopic clinic,
I saw the workings of my entrails
Reflected on a screen.
Grievously I thought:
My mind, too, churns like that.

NORTH OF TWEED

The only time his money burned in his pocket
Was when he happened to be sitting
Too close to the electric heater.

CONCLUSION NOT LEAPED TO

Dogs, like ourselves,
Bark at what they don't understand.
But let it not be assumed
That either they or we
Understand everything not barked at.

BOREDOM

Whenever I asymptote
The estates of the mighty
I envy their thick shrubbery and tall fences,
And smile to think how often
Those who have attained this blessed privacy
Don't know what to do with it
When they've got it.

PASSAIC BIBLE

My friend the scientist said:
"I'll look it up in my Bible."
I was pleased by his unexpected piety,
Whereupon he drew out
A black liturgical volume, much tattered—
Kent's *Mechanical Engineers' Handbook*
(10th edition 1923, 153rd thousand,
Copyright by the Passaic National Bank and Trust).

DIALOGUE

"The moonlight hurts my eyes. Let's keep behind
The trees."
                    "It's not my eyes; it hurts my mind."

ULTIMATUM

Student of the Neverlasting Now
I know too well, necessity inveterate
Corrupts my vivid Present into Preterite.

O ultimate verb, so variously inflected,
Be unexpected:
As you Say When, allow
Just time for my Here's How.

AFTERTHOUGHT FOR ST. PATRICK

In respect of the recurrent emergence of the theme of sex, it must always
be remembered that his locale was Celtic and his season spring.

—JUDGE J. M. WOOLSEY, Decision on Joyce's *Ulysses*, 1933.

> He heard the clock its knell tick,
> He heard the blackbird sing:
> Reaction peristaltic
> And psychic too, they bring,
> For his locale was Celtic
> And his season, spring.

ANOTHER YEAR TO WAIT

While the Old Mandarin
Was trying to make up his mind
How to describe a dogwood flower
The dogwood season was over.

A LESSON

The path was strewn, one day last winter
With curly shards of clear ice,
Broken tubes of frozen rain
Blown from the trees.
I wanted to go out and study them again
To see exactly what they looked like,
But I didn't.
I try to teach myself,
We are given only one chance to see things.
We can't always go back for another look.

MASSACHUSETTS MODESTY

My favorite inscription lately
I saw blazoned
On the back of a grocery truck in Boston:—
DON'T COME TOO CLOSE
MAYONNAISE IS DRESSING.

EPITAPH

"I'm sorry," said the employer:
"I wanted to give your friend a job
But he smelled so strong of booze.
Of course that ruled him out, ipso facto."

"You mean dipso facto."

TWO THINGS

Two things are troublesome to me
And turn my warm blood cold:
The briefness of the dogwood tree,
The knowledge that there still will be
Full moons when I am old.
Then passively I realize
(With some surprise)
I would not have it otherwise.

GRAMMARIAN'S FUNERAL

The more I study the English language
(Said the perplexed old scholiast)
The more disturbed I get.
I learn from Bartlett's *Familiar Quotations*
That John Godfrey Saxe wrote
"This too will pass away"
And so did Warren Hastings, Nathaniel Hawthorne,
T. B. Aldrich, and Lanta Wilson Smith.
But, per contra, Paul Hamilton Hayne,
Theodore Tilton, Ella Wheeler Wilcox
And James Sexton Holme
All said
"This too *shall* pass away."
What will or shall I do?

A MAN I LIKE

He lives by stock-trading and steam heat
But he was raised in the country
And he can't read *Snow-Bound*
Without finding
(As Whittier said he would)
Tears in his eyes.

CAROL FOR STREET CROSSINGS

The light that's red as a holly berry
I find irritating, very.

The light that's green and bids me go
Pleases me like mistletoe.

I pay no heed to the light that's yellow
But leave that for the other fellow.

LISTEN TO THE MOCKING-BIRD

The laughter of scholars,
    Subtle, suppressed,
Is ill-paid in dollars
    And mostly unguessed.

Philosophers' laughter,
    Deep but not loud,
Is, many years after,
    Made shrill for the crowd.

PURPLE FADES SO FAST

Old carbon sheets! I hold them to the light—
   Impacted thin, and blurred,
I see the lines I wrote last night:
   Ghosts of the purple word.

APPOMATTOX

What do you want: fame? service? pelf?
A Pacifist? A Bitter-Ender?
What are your peace terms *with yourself?*
Unconditional Surrender!